Four Winds

Fredrick Hudgin

Novels

The End of Children Series:
    The Beginning of the End
    The Three-Hour War
    The Emissary
Ghost Ride
School of the Gods
Green Grass
Sulfur Springs
Old Dreams and Young Adventures (Short Story Collection)

Short stories

A Rainy Night
Ashes on the Ocean
Being Dad
Get Them OFF!
Nice Day for a Ride
The Chair
The Last Salute
The Longest Ride
The Mission
The Second Chance
The Wiz
They Don't Have Christmas in Vietnam
When Is a Kiss Not a Kiss

Poetry Collections

Four Winds

Fredrick Hudgin

Four Winds

This is a work of fiction. Names, characters, places, and incidents either are the product of the author's imagination or are used fictitiously, and any resemblance to actual persons, living or dead, business establishments, events, or locales are entirely coincidental.

Four Winds

ISBN: 978-1544609959

Printed in the United States of America

To the women and men whom I have loved.
I hope it was worth it.

Fredrick Hudgin

Poetry is when an emotion has found its thought
and the thought has found words.

Robert Frost

Table of Contents

Part 1

~

Poems Not About Love, Hurt, or Loneliness

15 Pisses in the Wind

Sittin' in a bar
Drinkin' beer after beer,
Watchin' everyone havin' fun,
Bein' friends to everyone but me.

All I do is watch my beer go down,
And listen to the Eagles.

"Sure, I'll have another."
Make that a life
or a wife
for the night
or two.

Would I be friends with me
If I saw me in a bar?

Bob Seeger helps resurrect friends
Who don't think of me anymore
And the whiskey in my glass helps
Bring back the good times
I'm sure we had once upon a time.

But all I really accomplish
Is to take 15 pisses.
I close my eyes,
And pretend I'm on Mt Rushmore
With my back to the wind.
At least I learned that much.

A Prayer
(Looking out at Concord Naval Weapons Station)

How soft they look
  covered in
The fresh green and
  wild flowers of Spring.

The wind caresses them
  with sun-warm breezes,
Pushes grass waves
  to lap at their base.

The fences, towers and
  patrols
Keep me from running
  barefoot
To play king-of-the-mountain
  under the puffy-blue sky.

Although that seems
  a better use of these mounds
Than to house
  hydrogen bombs.

Apple Pie

Hey, Joe, did ya hear?
My job is goin' away.
Some suits came down
From New York town,
And talked the whole damned day.

They talked about mergers,
Down-sizing, and ROI.
All those words
Said one damn thing:
"Son, you're out of a job."

Our business still made money,
Just not enough for them,
So they closed us down
In this one horse town
And took the jobs away.

Christmas's next month. Janie's due in March.
The kids need some winter clothes.
After fifteen years
Of workin' 8 to 5,
I don't know where to go.

Workin' midnights at the Quick Mart,
Goin' door-to-door all day.
Sellin' vaccuum cleaners,
And paintin' walls,
Hopin' for minimum wage.

At the ER late last night—
Josh's asthma's kickin' in.
Never seen so many

Four Winds

Hopeless people waitin'
In the Emergency Room.

I'd go down to Tacoma,
But the car's blown again.
Tuesday, the bank
Gave us thirty days,
Before they take our home.

At nights I wonder if I caused this,
By not workin' hard enough,
Or goin' on strike
For better pay
A year ago last May.

Lately I'm too tired to think,
Tryin' to make ends meet.
Ignorin' the pains
Inside my chest,
Until My Time comes for me.

Fifty thousand in term life
Is all there's left to give,
To some kids
Without a father,
To a wife without her man.

Fredrick Hudgin

Black Marble

They gather there slowly,
    once a year,
Products of death,
    of war, of fear.
They gather to wish
    like they gathered to die.
They draw us to them.
    We gather to cry.

So many names
    of men and boys,
Gone to the war,
    Gone to the skies.
Husbands and fathers,
    brothers and sons.
Heroes and villains,
    dead everyone.

We come to the wall
    by one and by many.
We come to the wall
    not sure why we're comin'.
We come to the wall
    to remember our past.
We come to the wall
    and cry for our best.

Those of us who lived
    to come back home,
Were greeted by anger,
    were greeted by stones.
We gave all we could
    when our country called.

Four Winds

"Do it for right".
        "Do it for God".

Now it's more
        than twenty years past.
Everyone says
        we're proud at last.
Our country smiles
        amid amnesty.
But they still haven't learned
        a God damned thing.

Our young men still go
        to fight in the wars.
They go to fight
        but don't know what for.
Your mother will know
        when they give her that flag:
You died for money,
        not some pretty rag.

Breath

Who would have thought that I would recognize it?
So many millions of breaths had preceded it,
In and out without thought or care.
Breaths taken in excitement.
Breaths taken in boredom.
Most taken without even a memory of their being taken.

Eventually it had to come,
For each beginning there is an ending.
In then out then ... nothing.

My heart cried out,
A moment of panic,
Then it too stopped.

I had hoped to hold the hands of my children,
Warm my wife's fingers one last time.
But dying, like birth, is a personal thing.
Alone we enter this life.
Alone we leave it.

Now Death comes for me.
Is he the Grim Reaper?
All cloak and scythe and boney hands?
Ready to cut my life away from this worn out body?

Or is he the ferryman Charon?
Guiding his boat over the River Styx,
And me without a gold coin.

Or is he St Peter, waiting at the gates to welcome me?
Heaven behind him, beckoning like a young woman,
Full of excitement and delight.

Or is death just ... Nothing.
Is the end just The End
Like before The Beginning?

All my life I've wondered about this moment.
And now I get to find out.
My last, or next, great adventure.

Fredrick Hudgin

Brotherhood

Three hours
 I've ridden my bike
  through the rain and sleet,
Three hours
 of endless cold,
Using the memory
 of my family
To guide me
 up this narrow road.

Three hours
 to think
  about the friends
Who have shared
 the other tire track,
Now gone
 to a careless left turn,
Or, worse,
 a three piece suit.

Memories of long rides
 on hot summer days
Fill my mind
 with warmth
  that I wish I felt.
The night slides by
 with only the wind
And my Harley
 to keep me company.

At the top
 of the pass
  overlooking our valley,
I can just see

Four Winds

　　our lights
　　through the rain.

The wind
　　is my friend,
And the bike,
　　my companion.
Three hours
　　we have shared
　　the communion of the road.
None of us
　　want this ride
　　to end yet.

One more moment
　　we pause,
Then the lights
　　draw us forward,
Like moths
　　to the sacrifice.

Fredrick Hudgin

Buffalo

Land of young people
      passing through,
For a month or a year,
      until college is done.

Old people
      living out their lives,
With memories of children,
      now somewhere else.

Shuttered buildings,
      potholes in the streets.
Noisy exhaust pipes,
      radios that make my walls shake.

People talking loudly
      to people sitting next to them.
So many cigarettes
      and pot's still illegal.

But the Bills are playing
      this weekend.
And there's a concert
      at the harbor.

Sailboats fill the lake
      leaning away from the wind
Some big, some small
      bouncing among the waves.

Canada awaits,
      just to the north

Four Winds

With vineyards, Toronto,
    and duty-free Scotch.

Stores on Hertle and Elmwood
    I haven't visited yet
Now I never will
    So sad – they looked interesting.

Young men with pants
    below their bottoms
Trying so hard
    to look like gangsters.

And they wonder
    why no one
Offers them
    a job.

No open Mic's
    to read my poems
To people who won't hear
    the things I've seen.

The only thing
    That remains to do.
Is pack my car
    and leave.

Without my bike
    that someone stole.
I hope it found
    a good home.

Another town
    I can talk about
In the past
    tense.

Fredrick Hudgin

Changes

When the end is looming ahead
dark and terrible
And the ghosts of your memories
haunt your smile,
Remember that each ending
is also a beginning
And each thunderstorm
has a rainbow inside.

Charlie, Lynn and I

Morning...I hurt.
The old scars from road rash and fights
    Are stiff and sore.
You're not twenty anymore, asshole.
    Just rest a while.

The faces of brothers past drift in front
    Of my closed eyes,
As I smoke the day's first cigarette.

There's Lynn comin' on to every pretty girl
    In every bar we ever went into,
Flashin' those white teeth and fillin' the room
    With his easy laugh.
Fell asleep in his cage after workin' two shifts for weeks
    Tryin' to give his kid a Christmas to remember.
Your boy got his first ride this spring, Lynn.
    We put it together while the snow flew.
He's got a woman with him, too.
    Loves her as much as she loves him.
Probably be setting up house together pretty soon.
    You should've been the Grampa instead of me.

There's Charlie with his gray hair and quiet wisdom,
    Always seeing the good in people.
Always believing we were better than we were,
    Even when we weren't.
Your lessons helped me through raisin' Lynn's boy
    Long after cancer closed your eyes forever.
Never knew you'd been to Nam until a color guard
    Showed up at your funeral.
Just like you to earn a Silver Star being a medic
    And not tell anyone.

Fredrick Hudgin

I hope you and Lynn have found each other over there
     And are ridin' with the Devil to the bar rooms of Hell.

As I pack the campsite onto my bike,
     I admire her lines and chrome one more time:
A painted lady covered with diamonds
     From the rain that fell just before dawn.
Charlie taught me to paint like this one winter
     When we were both out of work.
I know flames aren't your style,
     But even you might like these, old man.

One kick and she settles into her loping idle,
     As eager as me to find the road.
Just as we are about to leave,
     The sun breaks free of the clouds
And fills the campsite with a misty rainbow
     Of colors and shadows.
For one magic moment,
     Lynn and Charlie are with me again.
I feel their arms around my shoulders,
     And their approval in my heart.
I know if I breathe, the moment will be gone,
     So I just close my eyes and love them,
Silently sharing the magic of our brotherhood
     One more time.

Reality elbowed its way back into the meadow
     As the sun departed.
Our stolen moment together now a memory,
     To be placed gently with the others.
Without looking back, I ease my scoot out onto the highway
     And find that comfortable spot in her seat.
Soon the road is dancing under the foot pegs
     To the tune of her mighty exhaust.
The cobwebs of the night before
     Lie by the side of the road many miles behind,

Replaced by the expectation of a hot breakfast,
    And a pretty waitress,
And all the miles to go until Charlie, Lynn and I
    ride together again.

Fredrick Hudgin

Chasing Moonbeams

I took a trip
    from here to there
In the comfort
    of my rocking chair.

The fog flew with me
    for a while
Looking like skulls
    or a crocodile.

Canyons and valleys
    of monstrous fluff
Filling the sky
    with huff and puff.

Angry one moment,
    the next serene,
Then chasing a fairy
    up a moonbeam.

Above us all
    the moon holds court
Looking askance
    while we cavort.

His cold stone face
    above our fun
Never laughs or cries
    or tries to run.

He will never take
    a whimsical trip
Or know the glory

Four Winds

of a triple back flip.

He just watches and wishes
        and says "Someday..."
"Someday I'll go."
        "Someday I'll play.

But the plane is climbing
        drawing me on
With miles to go
        until the dawn.

Sliding on moonbeams
        and skimming the clouds
Is too much fun
        to be allowed.

One last moment
        let me play
Then up and up,
        away, away.

Looking back
        I hope to find
One more glimpse
        of faerie time.

But all I see
        is moon and clouds
Swirling, surging
        up and down.

Hiding the fun
        from all but me,
Making believe
        it was fantasy.

Clayton Club Saloon

Fresh paint covers the memories
That leak into the room
      like water into an old rowboat
Up through the floorboards
Bringing with it the ghosts
      of dusty Saturday nights.

The old piano's gone,
      playing off key
To an empty room
      at another hotel
      of one night dreams.

The cowboys no longer
      smell of the streams
      in the hills nearby,
And the horses that had been
      tied to the rail out back
Have been replaced by
      sports cars and
      mini vans.

But the music's the same:
      Willie Nelson, Waylon Jennings
      and such.
And I can still get a smile
      or a fight:
      my choice.

Some things change
      and some things don't.
Which is important depends
      on which way you see 'em.

Cleansing

The bag slowly swirls
    in the current
Back and forth among the reeds
    and stones.
The grocery store name
    on the side
Is blurred with dried mud
    and oil smears.
It can't break free
    of the duck's neck
While the flies land and leave
    the eggs of her demise

The duck was on migration
    with her mate
When they landed on this pretty
    island of water
She tried to swallow the tip of the bag:
    it looked like a frog,
All wiggly and green, then the bag got caught
    around her neck.
She struggled for two days trying to fly
    or swim or eat
Until she finally died next to her mate,
    gasping and desperate.

Each morning the sun rises
    upon the ruin of the stream.
The sewage from the farms and the factories
    and the city nearby
Lie like a pall on the ghosts of the things
    that used to live here,

Among sad memories of the ecosystem
      that once flourished bountiful.
The duck slowly rots with the chemicals
      and the garbage
And the carcass of any living thing
      unlucky enough to enter.

Hear the voice of the stream;
      it's calling to the Goddess.
"Cleanse me, mother."
      it cries.
"Take this cancer called 'people' away
      to the Hell that they've created."
I hang my head and cry
      to be part of the species
Who have created this monster
      and have no idea
How to heal the wound in the Earth
      that eats our childrens' future.

Cloud Love

Clouds are amazing all day long.
  Starting golden with the dawn,
Full of shadows and dreams fulfilled,
  Veiling the firs, hiding the hills.

Shades of pink and gray give way
  to the business of the day.
There's work to do! Out of bed!
  Rise and shine Sleepy Heads!

Crops to water and lakes to feed,
  Give a drink to birds and trees.
Make two lovers run for cover,
  Loving the music then each other.

Dusk slowly draws the covers of night
  pillows of gray replace pillows of light.
Then the cauldron bubbles high in the sky.
  The excitement boils and builds. Oh my!

Thor has come from Valhalla to play
  Thunderheads rise at the end of the day
Builds and throbs then begs for release
  Flash! Bang! Boom! And finally peace.

The air is charged after the fun
  The wind is sighing; the lightning's done.
Thor is sleeping in his stony attic
  And you thought lightning was merely static!

Fredrick Hudgin

Comin' Home

The plane slowly crawls across the sky,
      while I discuss OJ's trial with Jack Daniel's,
Or the fat, Italian, body builder, transvestite next to me,
      who needs half of my seat
      or just wishes he did.

The hours pass like the clouds below
      with more always ahead,
Giving the feeling of progress but accomplishing nothing
      but to get me drunk.

Sometimes I play a game like trying to remember
      what the kids will say,
Or pretend that my wife will kiss me
      like we'd just become lovers last night.

At night in the hotel room I pull the pillows around me
      so they feel like her when we used to sleep together,
A hotel infidelity of urethane and cotton,
      leaving the pile for the maids to ponder,
      if they give a damn at all.

Sometimes I buy a tape of kid's songs to play in the rental
car.
      "For the kid's." I tell the clerk as she slides it into the
bag,
An unknowing accomplice,
      aiding and abetting a closet kid song player,
      a felony at the least.

It usually takes a couple of days before coming home
      turns into staying home.

Dad

You and I were never friends,
Neither of us knew how to be.
That made our times alone together
Very special and cherished to me.

You drew me schematics when I was ten,
And found the parts in your hoards
Then I would build them and make them work
On mother's mahogany boards.

You taught me how to mow the lawn
And work outside all day,
Rejoicing in the smell of fresh turned earth,
Mixed with new mown hay.

I made up stories about your medals
That you got in world war two.
You were my hero and my Dad
And I was there fighting, too.

We attacked deep bunkers filled with men.
Tanks would flee on sight.
Alone, we beat those Nazi bums
Then relaxed on Sunday night.

Together, each Spring, we'd tour the state
With science projects spinning,
But found they wanted pretty and bright
Instead of just my thinking.

Christmas season of my senior year
Found me scared and pale.
I called at 10 on a Saturday night
From our city's lonely jail.

You had to borrow from Grandpa
Because no one would cash a check,
But Mom wouldn't let you leave me there,
With all those human wrecks.

Fredrick Hudgin

When I left college to join the war
In nineteen sixty eight,
I was finally going to be like you
And defend the American way.

God, I was proud, that first trip home,
'Cause I had a ribbon, too,
And a medal that said I could shoot my rifle
Nearly as well as you.

The only time I heard you cry
Was when I called to say
That I was going to Viet Nam,
Leavin' in a couple of days.

Somehow, I made it through that war,
And got my medals to wear
With memories of my silent dead
And our leaders who didn't care.

I wish I had written down
All the stories that you told us three
About your childhood in the South
And the squirrels in your pecan tree.

I knew all about being a father,
Before I became a Dad.
Then somehow things got changed around,
And your way wasn't so bad.

You see "Dad" is a special title
For men who love their kids,
Men who help them find *their* road,
No matter where it leads.

I'm sorry that my childhood
Was filled with so much pain,
But I had to go through all that
To get where I am today.

Four Winds

I love you for not giving up on me,
Or writing me off as "bad".
You'll always be my special hero.
You'll always be my Dad.

Fredrick Hudgin

Dreamin'

Sometimes as I tighten my verse
And make it so Spartan and terse
I dream of the past
When writing was fast
And I didn't know better from worse.

Dreams from the Lizard Lounge

She sat there one night all alone,
Tryin' to get her courage up.
He didn't understand at all,
Sometimes gentle's better 'n being tough.
If he'd touch her cheek softly
Or gently caress her breast,
She'd be with him now instead of us:
The world's rejected best.

And we come here to smile
And laugh for a while
And escape to our dreams.
Cause while we're here,
We're the best in the mirror
That we've ever seen.

Billy buys a round for the bar,
Smiles as we knock 'em back.
His wife is in Missouri
Says she's never comin' back.
He knows he should miss her,
Maybe even kiss her
And hug the kids.
But it hurts less to sit here drinkin'
Than it does to try again.

Somehow closin' time at the Lounge
Always comes too soon.
We trade in our shiny new dreams
For the ones that are comin' true.
Was it last week or last month
Or maybe even two
When the dreams we are runnin' from

Were the dreams we were runnin' to?

Easier

It's always easier
      to ask for understanding
Than it is
      to give it.

Fredrick Hudgin

Falling Leaves

Ten years ago
  a farmer planted all these trees
So they could grow
  in the sun and water
And they did that.

They were going to decorate
  peoples' lawns
And corporate headquarters
  and golf courses
But it never happened

For some reason
  the farmer sold the land
To a developer
  who finally decided
He would build.

Maybe it will be a church
  or maybe an office
Or maybe a swarm of
  little houses
Built too closely together.

But none of that matters
  to the trees today
As the backhoe
  with the huge claw
Tears them from the earth.

They shudder as it grasps them
  then crack and moan
As it rips their roots

Four Winds

loose from the soil
That fed them.

No more will they
        sway in the wind
No more will they
        change color in the fall
And begin their winter rest.

I watch them fall
        one by one
To be placed next
        to each other
Behind the back hoe.

Clutching each other
        one last time
Before they are carted off
        to the pulp mill
Following countless others.

The price of progress
        is the death of some things
Which yields the birth
        of others
And accomplishes nothing.

Except that I can no longer
        walk among those silent trees
And listen to the wind
        and the birds
Play among their branches.

I can no longer get relief from the heat
        in their shade
And hear them sing
        to each other

In my dreams.

.

Four Winds Ring

Four rings they are,
    woven like the winds,
Each one separate,
    yet part of the pattern
That none could make
    alone.

One ring blows soft,
    warm with love
    on moonlit beaches,
Full of wind in the
    palm trees and
The surf gently washing
    our feet.

One ring blows lonely
    from the deserts
    and battlefields,
Whispering the wisdom
    of the dead,
Silently watching
    as we pass.

One ring blows high
    from the mountain tops,
    telling tales
Of hopes and
    anguish,
Of where we're going
    and where we've been.

One ring blows cold
        from the ice
        and snow,
Where wisdom and
        justice are
Two edges
        of the same sword.

A ring of love.
A ring of thought.
A ring of sight.
A ring of judgment.

Together now
        as we are:
Companions,
        lovers,
Teachers,
        mothers.

Together we approach
        the beginning and
        the end
 The birth of our
        future and
The death of our
        past.

We are one.

Fourteen Years Old

He must have seen me leave,
        followed me like a thief,
Pressed his knife against my neck
        then threw me to my knees.

Limp. I lay there in the mud
        looking at the trees,
Whispering quietly over and over:
        "Please don't, please stop, please..."

It hurt when he entered me
        and I tried so not to cry,
But he saw my tears, my sobs held in,
        then I saw him smile.

After a while I went away
        and let him do as he wished.
He couldn't hurt me where I was,
        escaped on a rescue wish.

I went to a place called Happy
        about which little girls know,
With meadows, birds, a mountain stream,
        and, of course, a big rainbow,
A place to run and laugh and sing,
        but never a place to cry,
Where Daddies love their daughters
        and Mommies never die.

He was gone when I returned
        lying there crushed in the rain.
People whispered how dirty I was
        when I came back to the dance again.

I told them I'd fallen in the storm.
        Please help me. Take me home.

And only thirty minutes I'd been gone,
    so many lifetimes ago.

I put my clothes in the trash
    and washed the dirt away.
Now the hot water is gone again,
    but the dirt, it still remains.

Daddy would call me names
    and hit me if he knew
Then he'd scream and hit his wife,
    'cause that's what Daddies do.

Hug me, Teddy, hug me hard,
    while we watch the moon,
Little girls should be skipping rope
    not growing old this soon.

I think I'll take a walk outside
    and hide my tears in the rain.
Maybe I'll find a place to hide
    so I can cry with God again
For the little life inside me
    that grows more each day,
A life that shouldn't be there,
    to want, to love, to care.

Tomorrow's just another day,
    a day to take a walk,
Before people start to whisper
    and ex-friends turn to gawk,
We'll walk together, she and I,
    to the other side of town,
To the second floor above the alley,
    behind Wilson's Formal Gowns.

It's where they end babies' lives
    before they really start,
Far from doctors, nurses and caring,
    they'll cut out her tiny heart.

Four Winds

I wonder about the other women
    who came to that place
And how many died there on the table:
    a name without a face.

I wonder about the fathers
    and if they care at all
About the mothers they abused
    to meet their animal call.

He waits for me when I sleep,
    when I dare to close my eyes.
When dawn finally drives him away,
    I'm too damned tired to cry.

I see his eyes, feel him on me,
    sweating, grunting and leering.
I can't move. I can't scream.
    He'll be there when I'm dying.

I'm sorry, Daddy, I'm so sorry,
    that I was so young and pretty,
I'm sorry that I was where he was,
    I'm sorry I made a baby.

Daddy, I wish you could hold me,
    and whisper silly things
And be all the things that Daddies should
    until the school bell rings.

The bell that rings tomorrow,
    will toll her funeral.
I have to kill my firstborn child,
    tomorrow after school.

Today, I wish that just one time
    I could sit upon your lap,
My head resting on your chest
    my arms around your back.

Fredrick Hudgin

I'd listen to your quiet breath,
  your heart slowly beating,
And not think about Tomorrow
  until Tomorrow comes for me.

Maybe I'll die with her
  and together we'll escape
To that place that little girls know
  and no one's heard of rape.

Freedom

All the men want her,
Think they can have her,
They watch her closely
And buy her a drink.
They sense her freedom
Wish they could have it
Think they can buy it
For the price of a drink.

But you can't buy freedom.
It comes from inside,
Like joy and honesty
And beauty and pride.
Someday you'll find it,
Or it will find you,
But don't be surprised
If it hurts a bit, too.

Freedom can come easy,
To some it's like breathing,
Scares the hell out of people
That actions have meaning,
Makes them pass laws
"For the good of us all"
Or for the good us some,
As they draw the pall.

"How can you make money from
People that are free?"
"Exactly!" said the Senator,
"Vote for me."
"There" they cry.
"He looks so free."
I guess my long hair
Is finally a felony.

"Hey there cop!
He thinks he's free."
The Senator shouted,
Pointing at me.
It was an accident of birth,
I tried to explain,
I was born an American
On my birthin' day.

Like Thomas and Abraham,
Martin and John,
I believe that free men
Can decide right from wrong.
"Radicals, all of them."
he sputtered in rage.
"They'd all be in Attica.
If they were alive today."

Wait a minute,
I've got a right to be free.
I went to your Viet war.
What did it get me?
On unemployment
When I got home.
Kicked out of college
For hair too long.

How about you?
Are you scared of the pain?
Do you ever drop your clothes
And run in the rain?
Do you ever do *anything*
That's against the rules,
Even if they laugh and point
And think you a fool?

"Your Honor, Prosecution rests."
And the door slammed shut
Feeling like a coffin closing

and a fist in the gut.
"Whaddidyado?"
asked the child rapist one day.
"I was free." I said
And he moved away.

Fredrick Hudgin

Gifts

Everywhere I look
    are gifts.
Here let me share one
    with you.

Hold it gently.
    Isn't it beautiful?
See how it glitters
    and shines.

Wait.
    Don't go.
You forgot your gift.

I slowly turn your gift
    over and over,
Looking for a flaw
    but I don't see one.

Then I realize
    that you, too,
Have given me
    a gift.

God is Woman

I met God last night.
She was beautiful,
Not at all like I thought
        she would be.
I expected a wise old man
Or a glowing eminence.
She was blond
        and young
        and pretty.

We talked for hours about me
        and about her.
We laughed at our secrets
And cried at our failures
And she held me
And kissed me.

Her love filled me
        with awe
        and wonder.
I felt cherished
        and needed.

I tried to tell her all about
        why I did things
        and what I thought,
But she already knew.

And when she told me things
        I didn't understand,
My questions were answered
        before I said them.

Suddenly I was back in the world
        that I knew.
My lovely wife was beside me

asleep.
The birds were welcoming a new day.
I had an emptiness in me.
I felt like I had left a good friend
    after a long trip together.
I hadn't even said good-bye
    or thank you
    or I'm glad I met you.
Then a glow began in my tummy
    and I knew that she knew
    and that she loved me, too.

Grampa

Now that you're gone
    I wonder at the man you were.
A giant some say,
    a leader,
    a pioneer
    a teacher,
    a poet,
But to me you were just Grampa.

I remember you pushing me
    on your big rope swing
    until I could touch the leaves
    high above your head,
Pounding those stubborn rocks
    with a drop of sweat
    on the end of your nose,
Laughing at the little cuts
    on your legs from the rock chips,
Feeding Japanese beetles to the fish,
Cookouts with the crickets
    and the bullfrogs.

All those magic summers
    ended with my childhood.
I lost my innocence in Viet Nam.
    You lost yours in Las Vegas.
We could never go back
    to do it again.

Your decisions were not mine,
    but then mine were not yours,
And as much as I disagreed
    with some of the things that you did,
You were still Grampa
    and I loved you.

I'll miss your laugh
    that could fill a room,
And our hikes through the woods

to see the lupines,
The quiet evenings reading books
    and hearing tales of your exploits
    all over the world.

You were a giant among men,
    but to me you were just Grampa.

Growing Old

The rocks that I clung to
     in the turbulence of growing up
Are disappearing into Sand
     eroded by the progress of man
     as much as the forces of nature.

The people who guided those happy times
     are dissolving into dust,
One by one,
     as though they never were,
Leaving behind just memories
     or a headstone
To be brushed off
     on a Fall afternoon
When the colors in the trees
     and the smell of the forest
     says Winter is coming soon.

I miss my grandparents
     and those cool summer evenings
With the bullfrogs
     and the crickets,
Canoeing up the moon's reflection
     in the black glass of the lake.

The long hikes that we took
     from the Water Gap or
     the fire tower,
Meandering through hillsides,
     mountaintops, and meadows,
Have gone to join the other shades,
     slowly fading into oblivion.

Fredrick Hudgin

Why didn't someone tell me
          that old age hurts,
That people you love die,
That things built to last a lifetime
          wear out anyway.
That some mistakes
          can't be fixed.

We were sure that we would
          solve the world's problems,
That we were the good guys,
That we would finally find the way
          to right the wrongs.

Then we had babies
          and a house in the suburbs
And a minivan made more sense
          than a Camaro
And suddenly we are our parents
          and it's thirty years later.

Now, the politicians we used to attack
          are people we went to school with,
And the class bully is
          the town sheriff,
And our kids laugh at us
          for allowing it all to happen.

Hello Mom

Hello, Mom,
You don't know me.
I'm your daughter.
I'm going to grow up strong like you.
We'll share heartbreak and joys, wisdom and toys,
Then die while I hold you someday.

Our secrets will be whispered together,
While Daddy looks on, confused:
My first kiss, first love, our puppy, the Prom,
And that day when I'm pregnant like you.

You say it's your choice of the moment,
Not to have me by your side,
That times have got to be better,
Before you'll welcome my life.

That body you're growing inside you,
Will someday have beauty and grace,
And today they'll tear it to pieces:
You daughter, the awkward mistake.

When I chose you for my mother,
I'd hoped you'd choose me, too.
I'll wait for you to want me,
Until your babies are through.

Then I'll find another mother,
Who will love me and welcome me here,
And all things we should be together,
I'll be with her instead.

Hello, Mom,
You don't know me.

Fredrick Hudgin

I'm your daughter.
I'm going to grow up strong like you.
We'll share heartbreak and joys, wisdom and toys,
Then die while I hold you someday.

Highway Mornin'

I feel like I've just
      been born.
Dawn is comin' with a
      bright new morn.

And I can't lie.

Can't sigh.

Feels good.

Kiss me.

High.

Fredrick Hudgin

Hold That Thought

So **s**hould ya, or
Could ya, or,
Come on, baby, would ya?

Look at it this way:
I'll be true tonight,
At least until mornin',
Which always comes
Without warnin',
And you're faced with
The Person lying beside you, or
Maybe inside you,
And you say,
Maybe I shouldn't have, or
Maybe I wouldn't have, or
God, I have to pee.

There's not much that can't wait
When you have to pee.

I Wish Mr. Rogers Was Here

"Another day, it's just another day."
The words appear with the sun,
But it won't be just another day,
Lives will end 'fore it's done.

And I wish Mr. Rogers was here
To tell me right from wrong,
Sayin' if I'm goin' to Heaven or Hell,
Takin' this weight before I drown.

Those kids and their friends that used to laugh
They won't be laughing when the sun goes down
They won't be laughing when they hear our guns.
They won't be laughing when they hit the ground.

Today is the day of atonement,
Today is the Day of the Reaper,
Today is the day I have prayed for,
Today is the day *they'll* be weepin'.

I never thought I'd do it,
The reality was make believe:
Cowboys and Indians, kids playing with guns.
Not a specter earnin' his keep.

But you see it wasn't really me,
Shootin' as they screamed.
It was someone else taking over my body,
Settlin' the score for me.

Fredrick Hudgin

I'm a Buzz Saw

I'm a buzz saw, baby.
I'm a buzz saw, baby.
I'm a buzz saw, baby.
I rips 'em when they're young
And splits 'em when they're old
I'm a buzz saw, baby.

So when you're ready to rock,
And when you're ready to roll,
When you're ready ta ready ta ready
        ta really rock and roll,
Come hear the buzz saw baby

I like to buzz the blues
And I like to buzz 'em cool
I like to buzz 'em all night long
        and make sweet love to you.
I'm a buzz saw baby.

I got a girl named Raye.
She sharpens my machine.
She screams my name into the night
        As she is buzzin' me.
I'm a buzz saw baby.

And when the night is done
And the dawn is break' blue
You lay your head upon my chest
        and buzz me through and through
I'm a buzz saw baby.

In the Country

Back in the country.
     Been a while.
Been hangin' in the the city
     for far too long.

It's good to see again,
     things that I never see there,
Like corn rows in the dirt
     instead of in the hair.

And clean air in the air
     instead of my dreams,
The leaves litterin' the campsite
     and birds singing me to sleep.

Seems another world from
     McDonald's wrappers and beer cans,
Music that shakes the walls
     instead of bullfrogs at the falls.

Soul free,
     sets my soul free
To watch the sun
     Slowly set for me.

And the *stars* ...,
     there really *are* stars,
And they're making a movie
     just for me.

JonBenet

Good-bye, JonBenet,
Your song was much too short,
Discarded like a fragile vase
Lying broken on the floor.

I miss the little girl
With the sparkling blue eyes
Smiling in those pretty clothes
That made my daughters sigh.

We'll never know the woman
That you would have become.
You'll never meet your children
Or make love in the mountain sun.

The poems that were in you
To share with all of us,
Now lay silent in your heart,
Like paper turned to dust.

The future that you had
Was a shiny and wondrous thing:
Your first kiss, first love, college, Congress,
Then maybe the Presidency.

But now, all we have
Is a headstone with a name
Of a little girl who died too soon
And a prayer called JonBenet.

The Look-Away Girl

Maybe you've seen her walking alone.
She walks by here everyday,
Looking down, looking away,
Never has much to say.

Her world is different from yours and mine,
Like chalk on a blackboard in school,
Full of discord, out of focus,
Just reflections in a pool.

I wonder who loves her,
And why she looks away,
Where she calls home,
And if she'll smile today.

Does she pretend that her shining knight
Is coming back one day
From the war that claimed his soul
And sent him away to stay.

Or maybe the father she never had
Will love her from his grave
Instead of shouting at her everyday
"You're bad. You're evil. You'll pay."

I'd hug her, if she'd let me
And say that it's OK.
But she always turns away
When I approach her that way.

So I smile when she walks by
But she never meets my eye.
If her world inside throws her aside,
Why the Hell wouldn't I?

Fredrick Hudgin

Mornin' Dream Girl

I woke up this mornin'
        with your body on my mind.
You're a redhead, a blond,
        you're eighty or you're blind.
You've got big tits, little nips,
        fat or skinny, too.
You're my mornin' dream girl.
        Oh, God, how I lust you.

I was a boy of thirteen years
        the day that we first met.
I closed my eyes and felt my thighs,
        then took a gentle grip.
Somehow you knew just what to do
        to give me my release.
But then I had to figure out
        just how to wash my sheets.

I finally found a woman
        who smiled and spread her legs.
I broke a button, tore my fly,
        at least I didn't beg.
She was nice, a little plain,
        and her smile had lots of tin.
I just wish that I had waited
        'til I got it in.

Now I drift from face to face
        tryin' to find you.
No one ever feels as good
        as you and I can do.
You never tire all night long
        here or in far lands,
But you've got to fix one small thing:
        the callous on your hand.

Four Winds

I woke up this mornin'
    with your body on my mind.
You're a redhead, a blond,
    you're eighty or you're blind.
You've got big tits, little nips,
    fat or skinny, too.
You're my mornin' dream girl.
    Oh, God, how I lust you.

Fredrick Hudgin

Mothers

Mothers are an unlimited source of hugs and comfort.
They hold you when you're hurt.
They fix broken toys and always, always
Have fresh chocolate cookies to help heal skinned knees.

Mothers stay up late to type term papers,
When you're too tired to think anymore,
And drive you around your paper route,
Even when it's not really below freezing.

Mothers tell you when you're wrong,
And forgive you in the same breath,
Then tell you how you should have done it,
Then tell you to do it any way you want.

Mothers grow old sometimes
And serve diet Cokes with potato chips,
And show up for visits a day early
With presents they'd just found from last Christmas.

Mothers plant flowers in the Spring,
And mourn each one that dies.
When summer arrives, the survivors
Fill the yard with color and fragrance.

Mothers aren't supposed to die.
They are supposed to live forever,
Giving us unwanted advice that
We eventually decide we needed.

But mostly mothers aren't supposed to die
Because we miss them so much,
And never told them enough that we love them,

Four Winds

And we can't remember all the things they told us
When our children make the same mistakes.

Fredrick Hudgin

New York

Every morning I join the waves of commuters crashing
  on the steps of the escalators
As we rush from the warrens of the PATH trains
  to desks which anxiously await us,
Ready to spend yet another day
  climbing the walls of the concrete canyons
  to make money for someone else.

The sky I glimpse though the temples of Wall Street
  is full of clouds pregnant with rain,
Trying once again to wash the filth from the gutters
  into the filth from Albany.

Street people offer their paper cups like a chalice as I pass
  in which I place my penance
  for being part of the working class.

Construction workers lean on their shovels
  when the sewers grow tiresome
  or their beer bellies empty,
Parading their lust like peacocks
  for every woman to ignore.

A car alarm screams in ten flavors
  about a theft that never happened
  to people who don't care,
Echoing off the walls of the alley where it's double parked
  and the taxis use the sidewalk as a passing lane.

Working in New York is going to the zoo every day
  and seeing someone just like me
  looking back through the bars.
Thank God, for the locks
  and zoo keepers.

Night Heat

High heeled shoes
     and a camisole of lace
Painted lips
     with a killers face
Huntin' for love
     with your war paint on
Huntin' for scalps.
     Huntin' for fun.

C'mon baby,
     try to make me smile.
C'mon baby,
     make it hard a while.
C'mon baby,
     let me deep inside.
C'mon baby,
     let's take a ride.

Your hips move slowly
     to that primal beat,
Fillin' the room
     with your body's heat.
"Come get me, daddy,
     the time is right.
Your little girl
     needs a man tonight."

Now the dawn is here
     and your daddy's gone.
Once again
     you are so alone.
Your paint is wrinkled
     as you masturbate,

Until tonight,
    until escape.

Old Friends

Sometimes I get sad
Thinking of the friends
That I have driven away.

Sometimes it was words
Sometimes it was love
Sometimes it was hoping they'd stay.

At the end of the day
When the quiet reins
And a beer is my company.

I wonder how they are
I wonder where they've gone
And if they ever think of me.

Fredrick Hudgin

Our Home

Our home is quiet at last,
The bellowing and violence faded
Into memories that I wish I didn't have.

Questions start to float to the surface:
Why, what, when, who, where -
A Journalism 101 project.

"Just the facts, Mister"
I hear Joe Friday's voice say
From the time when I was young also.

If I puzzle it out, if I take the time,
If I look within, all will come clear,
The answer will manifest itself.

That's the promise of Mars:
Retreat into your cave and ponder.
All will be revealed.

But the Whole is still a hole
That no amount of pondering
Can fill.

A piece of me is gone,
Staying at a friend's house
Because she couldn't tolerate mine.

What kind of father am I
That my daughter flees our house
Leaving those foul words hanging in the air?

Four Winds

What did I do wrong?
Was it me or her
Or both, or neither?

Should I lay this on the altar of Menses
Or is it just part of being fifteen
Or of being fifty-five?

Kids should come with an instruction manual.
Parents aren't supposed to die.
I'm not supposed to get old.

Fantasies of a middle aged man
With a teenage daughter
Who ran away last night.

Fredrick Hudgin

Pele

So many sounds it took to get here:
>   the jet engines blasting us down the runway,
>   the jazz with coffee and breakfast,
>   the chattering as your bed came into view,
>   the car engine pulling us up the volcano to meet you.
So many sounds to get to here – to get to the silence where you
>   sleep,
>   only the bees and wind remain, playing the lullaby that is as
>   timeless as you.
They whisper of the glory of Pele when she wakes from her
>   slumber,
>   of the fire and rock that is both the beginning and end,
>   of the power of creation and the power of death.
I want to wander among the cinders and lava flows that fill your
>   bed now,
>   to put my hands in the dust and feel your power that still
>   lies beneath the ground
>   but that will have to wait until my next visit.
I picked up the garbage that the tourists left behind.
>   They didn't know any better, I was glad to help.
>   Thanks for listening to me listen to you.

Programmer's Lament

I am a computer programmer.
I am highly trained and highly educated.
My job is to find alternatives.
I do my job well.

You are my manager.
You expect me to question solutions,
    not lifestyles,
Programs, not dress codes.
I may be creative ...
    in programming ...
    from nine to five ...
    at my desk ...
    with short hair ...
    in a suit.

And you wonder why I question
    you, too.

Fredrick Hudgin

Requiem for Tom

It's quiet now.
The ambulances, the sirens serene,
To help someone else
On the flight path of ended dreams.

These hands that led countless babies
From their mother into the day,
Now lie broken and ruined,
Tools to be mourned then cast away.

A whole lifetime of memories
Have led me here,
A collage of snapshots
Of exaltations and fears.

I'll miss clocks ticking
And sunflowers in August,
Butterflies and coffee,
Hot baths and sage dust.

I'll miss holding my children asleep on my lap,
Walking hand-in-hand and taking a nap,
Watching your face when you smile asleep,
Reading Robert Frost when the snow gets deep.

But then people always see what's lost,
Before they see what's gained.
And I have miles to go,
Before I sleep again.

The Bear

Feel the change in the air.
Feel the energy, the power,
Undulating just out of sight.

This is a time of the looking-in,
A time of peace and growth.,

The wind is blowing,
Carrying the pulse of what will be,
      has been.

Guide me, brother.

Fredrick Hudgin

The Chair

This morning I walked into my living room
With a cup of coffee
And walked by an old chair
That was alone in the sun
By a window.

So I sat down for a few moments
And listened to the quiet of the house.
The girls were at school.
My son was off doing errands.

I closed my eyes
And let my mind drift
To all the memories
That this chair was part off.

I have a picture somewhere
Of my Grandmother holding me
Right after Mom brought me home
From the hospital.

She was sitting right where I am
With her elbows propped on these solid arms.
I was looking up at her with wonder.
I did that a lot around her.

And years later
when we buried Grandma,
I have a picture of my mother
Sitting here crying.

This chair has been home to countless feet
As we used it as a makeshift stool

Four Winds

Or as the major support for a blanket fort
And Saturday night sleepovers on the living room
floor.

When my first son was born,
Grandma and Mom took turns
Feeding him while they sat here.
And I slept the sleep of the dead.
Knowing he was safe in their arms.

Now this chair has come to my house
To be friends with the rest of my
Hand-me-down menagerie.
Mom and Grandma will never again
Hold a baby in their arms
While this chair holds them both.

I feel like I have stolen it,
Like the chair doesn't belong here,
Since they aren't here to be with it.
It should still be in their house instead of mine
And one of them will walk through the door in a
moment
Asking if I need another cup of coffee
Or if I need any help with that baby.

But that won't happen again
At least not in this lifetime.
I guess I will have to hold my childrens' babies
For Mom and Grandma
Until one of my kids gets to put this chair
Into their living room
And have a quiet cup of coffee
While they sit in the sun
And listen to their memories.

Fredrick Hudgin

The Eagle

There's the eagle again.
It's cry is unmistakable,
        raucous and harsh,
Makes people uncomfortable
        and angry.
They don't understand.

Come with me,
        it calls.
Fly with me
        to the sun.

No hesitation,
        I spread my wings.

What a feeling
        to soar aloft together
        after all those years.
Flying together,
Knowing where each other is
        by instinct and trust.

Until the flight
        is done,
I will revel
        in the joining of spirits.
No regrets,
        the past will lose itself.

Fly on, brother eagle,
        I will follow.

The Flight of the Eagle

So many years have passed
While I looked down,
        waiting,
        watching,
Enjoying my peace,
        the rushing wind,
        the freedom,
        the solitude,
Living each moment with wonder
        and awe,
Growing,
        always growing.

Now you've come to fly with me
Having fought the same battles,
        fears,
        doubts,
Embracing your fears,
        attacking them,
        enjoying them,
Sharing each moment with each other,
Knowing,
        but not knowing why.

We will fly together forever,
Seeking new horizons,
        new gifts,
        new insights,
Giving the power,
        receiving it,
        growing it,
Waiting until the other eagles
        find us - find them,

Fredrick Hudgin

Flying,
        always flying.

The Goddess

Someday you'll be gone
    or I'll be gone.
How will I live without you?

How will I explain
    to my children
    That you are not with me, too?

What will I do
    when I see something you'd like
    And you're not beside me?

Who will hold me
    when I cry
    And tell me how it should be?

Who will give your daughter
    a ride on a Harley
    On a hot summer day?

What will you do
    when you see something I'd like
    And I'm not on the way?

Will you think of me
    when you're with your lover
    And you close your eyes?

I'll feel your nails
    as you scratch his back,
And you will hear my sighs.

In magic we are one.
    Hear the magic call.
    The Goddess is laughing at us.
    She does that.

Fredrick Hudgin

The Living Room

Shadows between the cedars
      fill with a passing cloud.
A lonely coyote
      calls to it's family.
A crow shouts a challenge
      as it crawls across the sky,
While the wind whispers
      for me to leave.
I am an interloper,
      no matter what the deed says,
Trespassing in the living room
      of the Goddess.

The Meadow

I remember when you ran
    through this sunny field,
Your eyes full of wonder
    that three year olds see.

The grass was so tall
    that I could only see
The sun on your hair
    with the pollen and the bees.

We chased butterflies and grasshoppers,
    and flew with the birds
Then explored an old ruins
    that was heavy with years.

I thought you would like
    to be buried here today,
To be guarded at last
    by such mighty days.

The noise of that war
    is far, far away.
They can go to Hell.
    You're home to stay.

Fredrick Hudgin

The Teacher

A teacher is someone
who adds color
To the black and white
of text.

The Two Sides of Traveling

These things are a bummer:

Missing the comfort of my own place.
Waking from a dream of kissing your face.
Wishing old friends could be her with me.
Getting a bed but paying a fee.
Seeing a sunset without my lover.
Walking in the rain far from cover.

These things are cool:

The excitement of a new country.
Unknown adventures at every corner.
The joy of making new friends.
Sleeping under the stars while the wolves cry.
Seeing a sunrise that brings goosebumps.
Walking with the rain in my face.

Fredrick Hudgin

To Dad

You weren't supposed to get old.

You were supposed to stay healthy
and play ping-pong
and tell me I was making mistakes.

Now you don't recognize me sometimes
and I have to change your shorts
when you have an accident.

I was so angry when I was young.
I used to think that you weren't a good Dad,
That you weren't there when I needed you.

Everything that was wrong with my life
Was always, somehow, your fault.
But it wasn't, of course.

And, now, instead of wishing
That you had been a better father,
I wish that I had been a better son.

Was I there when you needed me?
Will I be there when my son needs help?

Now I can hold your hand
without your pulling away.
And help you walk
When you have a mind to try.

When I was a boy
I pretended to be asleep
And you kissed me
On the forehead.

Four Winds

It wasn't until you were old
That I was able to kiss
You back and tell you
I loved you.

Goodbye Dad.

Tonight

Tonight is filled with a wind
Than blows hot in a young man's veins:
      warm and cold,
      relaxed and tense,
      filled with adventure and sex.

Breasts and muscles are paraded proudly
Swaying to the Latin music.
      The women look alluring
      and the men look tough,
      like the music filling the air.

Old women on bicycles,
Young men with dogs,
      non can escape
      the rhythm of the night.

It's a night to be part of,
Not look out at,
      a night to feel and remember
      and maybe to regret
      tomorrow

It is on a night like this
That visions are seen,
      lovers won,
      lives lost.

The world will change
For those it touches.
      Better stay inside
      or ...
      maybe not.

Travelin'

Ain't nothing like the bliss
    of a hug and a kiss,
When my daughter welcomes me home.

She scolds me for staying,
    She's sure I was playing,
And next time she won't let me go.

Someday she'll be gone,
    And I'll be at home,
Wishin' her here with me.

Wth mem'ries of the times
    she'd laughed and she'd
cried,
An old man's last company.

Waiting at the Faire

How like a fete it seems: gift shops and food stands,
  pretty colors and flags and carpets,
Lot's of smiles from people,
  there to help
While they push our loved ones
  away on a gurney.
"Just routine" the doctor says.
  "Be done before you know."

The children are playing
  quietly
As children do
  sometimes.
Toddlers proudly teetering
  from their mother to an aunt.
"Go fish!" commands another
  to her brother.

I hope the bullets they use
  are smarter than the ones I used in Viet Nam.
I hope they know the difference
  between the good guys and the bad guys.
'Cause people fight and die here
  just like we did:
A World gone insane
  while everyone pretends Normal.

I want to dig a fox hole
  and fill sandbags.
I want to attack some unseen enemy
  that is trying to spirit you away.
I want to watch it die slowly
  at the end of my bayonet.

Four Winds

And hope it does more good now
    than it did then.

We have to trust cures that didn't exist last year.
    When doctors told us:
"Just routine. Be done before you know.
    So much better than what we had last year."
And next year?
    Will they say the same thing?
To a captive audience with no one else to trust,
    While they watch their future leave on a gurney?

I want to grab the doc by the lapels
    like I did my platoon sergeant:
"Tell me it'll be OK!"
    I scream at the dream.
He turns to me slowly
    and smiles:
"Just routine. Be back before you know.
    Why don't you go get some lunch?"

Waiting

She lives her life in search of him,
Waiting for his touch, his voice,
Desperately wanting him to fill the void
In her heart, in her body, in her life.

She hears their children in the quiet night
Crying out to be born,
Wanting to start their life together,
"Please, Mommy, don't wait too long."

When will he come?
Where will I be?
How will I know
He's right for me?

Will he give me flowers on a rainy day
For no reason at all
And hold me close when I cry at night
Until the storm is gone.

Will he look past this shell I wear
To see me hiding inside
To see our love, the future we'll share
That will last until we die?

I hope he finds me before I'm old
While my beauty is still alive
To give him joy and bring him home
To my arms, my lips, my thighs.

And when our fire has cooled below,
From white hot to ember warm,
Our love will continue to glow all night,
Protecting us from the storm.

Welcome the Reaper

Blood wound slowly
       down her neck,
Pooling slightly
       on her breast
Then on to join the rest
       on the floor,

Blood which should
       be nourishing
       an unborn child
Or pounding with excitement
       at a mountain sunrise.

Still they used
       her body,
Again, and again,
       not content,
Their destruction
       not yet complete.

Sleep, my child.
They can't hurt you
       anymore.

Part Two

~

Poems About Love, Hurt, and Loneliness

A Friend

Remember this,
    woman of light,
When tossed about
    by storm and wind,
When everyone else
    has taken flight,
My port is safe,
    I am your friend.

A Word

When I tell my parents
    how I really feel
And they give me
    a hug and a kiss anyway.

When my son
    makes his bed
Just because he knows
    I wanted him to.

When I cry
    with my friend
And he cries
    too.

When I tell you
    I love you
And you just smile
    and love me back.

Beware of Restaurants in the Night

Why did you have to be there?

Why couldn't you have been somewhere else
       that particular night?

Why couldn't you have been
       wrapped in a lover's arms
Instead of smiling at me
       when I walked through the door.

Damn you.

I'd almost convinced myself
       that I didn't love you anymore.

Fredrick Hudgin

But You Know

I love you, but you know.

I like saying the words,
Feeling them start deep inside
And just as they leave my mouth,
I caress them one more time.

If I say them very softly,
It's almost like a kiss
From my spirit to yours.

Until I see you again
I will cherish the moments we've had
And send these words to you.

Clothes

I miss you.

Last week
    I wouldn't have said that,
But I had to fold your clothes this morning,
    and each piece of cloth
Told me its memories of our love.

You have better speak to
    some of them.
Everyone knows that
    silk blouses have no shame,
But your underwear were positively brazen.

Fredrick Hudgin

Come Fly with Me

I want to take you to a place you've never been.
I want to unlock my doors and let you in.
I want you to see my world from the inside out.
I want you to feel my pain, my love, my doubt.

Do you still want me?

I want you to love me
Like you've never loved before.
I want you to need me
And unlock all my doors.
I want you hold me
'Til the dawn draws near.
I want you to stay here
'Til you've cleansed my fears.

Come fly with me

Let me take to you to the sun
To that place where I run
When the world crashes around my head
And I'd be better off dead
Then you fill me with love
No matter what I've done
And I realize
It's OK to cry

Let me take you there

Confessions

I'm glad you
       don't want to be
Lonely anymore,
    either.

Fredrick Hudgin

Echoes from a Bell Jar

There. She's looking at me again.
Caught in the act of sneak peeking.
Both of us cowering behind the felony
Of our broken loves.

Are you *the* one?
Or are you just another one?
Does it matter tonight?
Does it matter anymore?

All that's left of the pyre
That we created when we met
Are just ashes that still warm slightly,
Until they, too, fade to black.

A passing shoulder is
Better than no shoulder.
Maybe it will be enough to last
Until the next false dawn.

Embroidery

I remember when I first held you
And looked into your eyes.
Mine were full of wonder.
Yours were kind of high.

Our love is the adhesive
That makes our lives whole,
Siamese twins joined at the heart
Two spirits with one soul.

I see you in every mountain sunrise
In every babbling spring.
I point you out to all my friends
But they don't see a thing.

I hear you in the whispering pines
High on forested hills,
And in the desert each sparkling night
As the earth grows dark and still.

I like to weave words of you
Because they're magical things
That can bring up memories we've never had
And places we've yet to see.

I can gaze down on the tops of clouds
And remember out future together
Then imagine our past that's gone so fast
Through calm and stormy weather.

But the present is really the part
That I love about you most,
Holding your hand, walking in sand,
Kissing and holding you close.

Everything

There, I've seen something
    you should have seen.
It was beautiful.
    It was ugly.
It was tender.
    It was brash.
It was intense.
    It was bland.
It was everything that
    I'll see for the rest of my life.
And you weren't here.

Why?

Every Time

Every time I see a sunrise,
  I wish you were there
  to see it with me.
Every time I hear the wind,
  I wish you could
  hear it also.
Every time I taste a new food,
  I wish you could
  taste it with me.
Every time the wind brings me
  something new to smell,
  I wish you were there too.
Every time I hold
  a bird just learning to fly,
  I send it to you.
Every time you try to hurt me,
  I smile and try
  to send you back love.
Every time I remember your lips
  and how they tasted
  when we kissed,
  I cry.

Favorite

One of my favorite
      things to do
Is to close my eyes
      and watch you.

Flyin'

I spend lots of time flying,
       looking down at the world,
       hearing the quiet and the peace.

We fly well together.
       I was surprised that you could,
       that you wanted to with me.

Two spirits,
       lost and lonely,
       in search of childhood dreams.

Now it's time to land
       and pretend that dreams end
       when you wake.

But, for a moment, we were one,
       soaring aloft together,
       knowing but not knowing why.

Fly free, little one,
       That's what dreams are for.

Fredrick Hudgin

Getting Ready

They really hurt,
      those young days,
When I was sure I'd die
      of a broken heart.

We were both just trying
      our wings,
Playing at being
      in love.

Why couldn't we have played
      at crying, too.

Ghosts

I saw your hair today.
It was in a bar,
But someone else
Was wearing it.

It made me wonder
Where you are,
How you're doing,
Who you love.

So many questions ...
That was the way it went with us.
I hope you found your answers.

Me?
I miss you.
So what else is new?

Fredrick Hudgin

Going Home

And now it's time
      to go home.
The car is silent and comforting,
      like a tomb.
A time machine to transport
      between now and then.
 I guess I'd rather
      be alone
      with now
Than go home and
      be alone
      with her.

Goodbye Sheri

The battlefield has grown
    silent and forbidding,
Littered with the ghosts
    of dead memories.

I weep as I wander among them
    and remember each happiness,
Now lying twisted and abandoned
    among the wreckage.

There is the first time
    we made love.
Over there is a tender touch
    in the middle of the night.

On the day we got married
    your high heals
Kept sinking into the new sod
    Mom put in our back yard.

I didn't know until later
    that I had been rubbing your butt the
    whole time.
While the minister lead the ceremony
    but everyone was watching my hand.

Here is the birth of our son.
    Oh what a day that was!
It didn't take long before we figured out
    that kids are a lot of work.

Fredrick Hudgin

The girls came one by one
    as children usually do
Amid hopping around the country
    on one adventure after another.

There is Jennifer graduating from college,
    She worked so hard,
Going to college, having a baby and getting
    married
    all at the same time.

And Katie enlisting when soldiers were
    dying every day.
Anxious to get to a war zone so she
    could do some good for the world.

Twenty two years of loving
    crying, growing
Laughing, traveling down
    our path together.

Only to have it end before the end.
    I wouldn't move to Florida
You wouldn't move to Washington
    You thought the rain would kill you.

I hope you found some happiness
    living with your friends.
Living a life without me to whine
    about your cigarettes and romance
    novels.

I will write down every story
    I remember about you
So our grandkids will remember
    you too.

Good Morning

I woke up this morning
    with some really weird vibes.
I feel like you're hurting,
    not physically, but spiritually.
I wanted to give you a big hug
    but you weren't here.
So this is the best I can give you right now.

Crawl up into my spiritual lap
    and let me comfort you.
Let me smooth your aura
    with my fingers.
Let me whisper in your ear
    and stroke your hair.
I love you.

No matter where we are
    or what words have been said between us,
    That will never change.
    That is my decision, not yours.

And there is nothing, good or bad,
    that you can do to change that.
You said that you have never become
    friends with a lover.
I have.

Maybe that is one thing that
    I am supposed to teach you.
Not how to do it,
    but that it can be done.

Fredrick Hudgin

Healing

There are a lotta tears around
    these days.
Yep. This is definitely the season
    for tears.

Sometimes they kinda creep
    up on ya,
Catch ya unawares doin' laundry
    then WHAM.
They gotcha.

Other times they're much more
    subtle.
They let ya get warm and cozy
    with a book,
    soft music,
    a glass of wine.
Suddenly it's rainin'
    on the paper
And ya don't care.

Then they really come down,
    like a summer shower,
Fast and furious,
    pounding down the old flowers,
    feeding the new ones.

Finally, when the thunder stops
    and the sun breaks through,
Your memory hurts a little
    less.

I Knew

I knew you were coming,
      felt our paths ready to meet.
I could see your face,
      feel your body next to mine,
A shade of what was to be,
      what was before.

I knew you were coming
      but I didn't know that
You were here
      until you kissed me.

I forgot to tell you
      all the things I've learned,
since the last time
      we loved each other,
Forgot to ask
      where you've been
And what truths you've
      found along the way.

But there's time for that
      later.
For now, just hold me
      and kiss me.
Our minds can say
      hello
After our bodies are
      through.

Fredrick Hudgin

In the Clouds

This is a morning for lovers,
    soft and foggy.
The coolness of my shoulder
    yearns for your cheek.

Sleeping alone is
    lonely, but
You song is
    in the birds, and
Your fingers are
    in the wind, and
Your kiss is
    in the sun, and
Your love is
    in my heart.

That will hold me until
    I see you again.

Into the Sun

Your eyes really do
     shine as much
     as I remember, and
The thank you
     kiss and hug
     good-bye will last
Until the next time,
     somehow.

I was afraid
     you'd see the
     longing in my eyes,
Afraid you'd ask
     me to go if
You knew how much
     I wanted to stay.

He's lucky,
     you're new man.
     I hope he knows.
He's still making
     the memories
     that I cling to.

Fredrick Hudgin

It Was Easy

Saying good-bye
     was easy.
We met for that
     last time,
Said that we
     both knew,
A polite kiss
     then a hug and
     no tears.
It was over,
     after all.

I keep finding
     the places
     we met and
Seeing new things
     that you
     would like.
I never knew
     so many people
     had your hair,
Or drove
     your car.
And I walk the hills
     in the moonlight
Because it's peaceful,
     not because
     we did it together.

I'm glad saying "Good-bye"
     was easy.
Now I have to learn
     how to say
     "I don't love you."

Later

Not meeting you tonight
    is ok.

We'll meet the next time,
    or the next,
When you don't have
    a spirit to help
Down their path.

I'll be ready when you
    get there, but
You'll probably
    be waiting
    for me

Leaving

I have to leave now.

I love you, but
      you know that.
You can give me
      encouragement, and
Lift me up
      when I fall, and
Cry
      when I fail.

But I have to leave because
      it's my path, and
You can't walk it
      for me.

Listen to the Wind

I came to see you tonight.
I was going to say:

That we didn't' have
                    any future ...
That we had to stop
                    before it was too late ...
That I loved you ...

We were supposed to make love
                    one last time.
I had it all figured out.

But you weren't there.

I'm so glad.

Fredrick Hudgin

Morning

I feel like crying.

Your head is quiet
      on my shoulder,
Your lips still smiling at
      the memory of
      last night.

The sun from
      the dawn
Lights up
      your hair
As the birds
      serenade us
      one last time.

I feel like crying but
      it will keep.
There'll be time enough
      for that
      after you're gone.

My Gift

I love you.

You don't have to earn it,
 or change,
 or be worthy,
 or love me back.

I love you.

Not the person
 you pretend to be
Or the person
 you want to be.

I love the little girl
 inside you
Whom you spend
 so much time protecting.

That's who I love.
 and that's forever.

Fredrick Hudgin

My Wife, My Lover,
My Soulmate, My Other

I'll never forget the first time we met.
God I wanted you.
Not like a lover, not yet.
I loved your hair,
I loved your face
I loved your body
        and your clothes.

At least I thought I did.
I tried so hard to impress you,
To act so collegiate and debonair.
But it didn't work.
I wasn't ready
And neither were you.

It wasn't until two more years had passed
That we met again.
At the right place,
At the right time,
Or maybe just the right us.

I had to learn that there's more to loving
Than getting married and having fun,
That it hurts when you're discarded,
That love is like a pitcher of water:
The more you put in,
The more you get out.

That was seventeen years ago
And I'm still finding new ways
        to love you.

I love you when you call me.
I love you when you worry that
        I'll find someone else.

Four Winds

I love you when you buy me clothes.
I love you when when I have to leave
    and you kiss me with your tongue

I love your hugs.
I love your smiles.
I love you when you talk about our children.
I love you when we watch them play.

But most of all,
I love you.

When we're old and fat and our teeth are gone,
When we smell bad and can't remember,
I'll love you.
Because loving you is as
Much a part of me
As me.

Nothing Really

Nothing really to say.

Just that I liked having you next to me
     last night.
And kissing you goodbye
     when you left.
And smiling each time I thought of you
     today.

I love you.

Or Did I Dream It

Here we are
    caught between the sky
    and the earth,
A Neverland that only exists
    when we are together.
Turn left at the second star
    then on 'till morning.
It's the stuff dreams are
    made of.
But dreams can come true,
    if just once in a lifetime.
All you have to do is believe,
    believe in fairies.
Everyone say it
    "I do believe in fairies!"
Someone told me that
    or did I dream it?
I met you once,
    or did I dream it?
I loved you once.

Petals

I always thought that
　　　　it's not OK to need anyone.
That when you want to reach out,
　　　　you're being weak.

But I want you to hold me, and
　　　　tell me you love me, and
Somehow, that doesn't feel weak to me.
　　　　It feels whole.

Problems

But that leaves another problem,
      because I love her, too.
She is a part of me
      that hasn't grown up yet.
And you are a part
      that has.

You feel the sun go down
      and
Hear the Grand Canyon
      and
Smell the Tetons.

She knows where I hurt
      and why.

Promises

It was a long time ago
When your mother lay dyin'.
She held my hand softly
To keep me from cryin'.
But there was steel in her voice
As she whispered to me,
"You take care of my baby.
You love her for me."

You are my lady.
You are my life.
You are my lover.
You are my wife.
I love how you hold me,
How you kiss me,
How you scold me.
I love that you chose me
For the rest of our life.

Now our lives are full
Of Brownies and ball,
Of asthma and chicken pox
And scrapes from a fall.
I see her in their face
When they run to you,
Lovin' the sun and the wind
And the clouds in the blue.

Our bodies aren't as young,
As they were back then.
We've got some wrinkles
And there's gray peeking through.
I wish she was here,

Four Winds

But I'm sure she'd approve
Of the woman you've become
And the paths that you choose.

Rain

The clouds are low today, dark with memories
Of what has been.
It's been a long ride from Heaven to Hell
And it surely feels like rain.

The house is quiet with the noise of us
As I enter our bedroom,
With our last words still hangin' in the air
Like a pall inside the gloom.

And the wind is startin' to blow,
Fingers against the window pane,
Pointing at the shame of our happiness
Slowly dying in the rain.

There's nothing left but tears
As they sing their silent refrain.
It's a long, sad song,
And the music sounds like rain.

Sometimes you have to let someone go
Before they can stay.
But "sometimes" never applied to us
And I think it's gonna rain.

Yeah, here comes the rain.

Reading

I can't read my poetry
    about you out loud,
My feelings keep getting
    in the way of the words.

Fredrick Hudgin

Regret

When we woke up
     together,
I could see it
     in your eyes.

You tried hard
     not to let it show
With smiles
     and kisses,
But it was there with us
     as you dressed.

All that I have left
     of our night together
Is our warmth
     amid the covers
Until that, too,
     fades.

Even last night
     wasn't worth
Losing all of the tomorrows
     that will never be.

Remembering

I remember each curve and
    hollow
    of your body,
How it tastes
    and smells.

I remember how my lips
    felt when I
    kissed each part,
The different textures.

We spent a whole night
    rejoicing in each
    other.

Remembering you is almost
    as much fun as
    loving you is.

Fredrick Hudgin

Renee

Your eyes sparkle
and your breasts wiggle.
It's so much fun
when you laugh.

Rhyming

I've been trying
     to make up a poem
     for you, but
All the words keep
     coming out the same.
They keep sounding like:

     I love you.

Sadness

Sadness slips over me
    like a pall.
I feel it cover my smile
    with emptiness.

It is a feeling like
    all others,
One to be enjoyed
    and learned from.

I remember other times
    when it came,
When I needed a teacher
    to ease the pain.

Hello, old friend.
    I've been waiting for you.

Sailin'

It was a Magic day from the start
      of clouds and sky and sunshine
When we went sailing, hand in hand,
      on the Harbor of Nursery Rhymes.

The wind blew your hair around your face,
      like springtime as a child,
Kicking up whitecaps in your eyes
      that showed every time you smiled.

I reached for you as you reached for me,
      two sailors lost and lonely,
Sailing their ship to the Land of Happy
      on the Sea of Broken Dreams.

We made a blanket boat, like children do,
      with cannons, swords and sails,
And sailed the seas to search for pirates
      and dragons to imperil.

We fought back the monsters that came to feed
      on the happiness filling our sails,
And laughed at the spray that washed away
      their battered monster tails.

The cove we chose to end our trip
      was a safe and happy place,
Sadly, we entered the portal back
      to rejoin the human race.

You gave to me your heart to hold,
      knowing I'd keep it safe.
It's safely anchored in our cove
      rocking in the waves.

I trusted you to keep my heart,
      I gave it forevermore.
It's yours to help you fight your dragons,
      with love and smiles and roars.

Secrets

I heard a secret today.
There I was in the men's room
    doing what men do
    in the men's room.

All right, so I was washing my hands
    but I still heard a secret.
This guy was talking to the mirror
    and telling it that he loved you.
And everyone laughed
    but he didn't even seem
    to notice.
Imagine that.

Sheri

Good-bye, Sheri,
Your song was much too short,
Ending like a fragile vase
Lying broken on the floor.

I miss the smiling woman
With the flashing hazel eyes
With all those pretty clothes
That made every woman sigh.

We'll never know the person
That you would have become.
You won't hold your grandbabies again
Or meet those yet to come.

The adventures that were in you
To share with all of us,
Now lay silent in your heart,
Like paper turned to dust.

The future that you had
Was a wondrous and shiny thing:
Kids, Christmas, and birthdays
And wondering what to bring.

But now, all we have to hold
Is a memory with a name
Of a woman who died too soon
And the end of all her pain.

Fredrick Hudgin

Sheri's Poem

I remember what he smells like
    most of all -
A carefully guarded memory
    reserved for late night mourning
When all hope of sleep or even rest
    has long fled
Down the corridors of loss,
    remorse and despair.

What a tease it was to see him
    in the clothes
That he once wore when
    we were together,
When I still clung to the hope
    that we would weather
This latest storm in the hurricane
    of our love.

A house isn't much to
    hold on to:
A sad second best to the arms
    of my lover,
But it's all I have left of the pyre
    that we created
Until it, too, joins the ashes
    in the wind.

Will he ever ask me to walk
    with him again?
Would I let him open those
    doors again?
How could I, when even the thought
    of forgiveness

Four Winds

Makes me weep on the floor
   like a pile of discarded clothes.

The pain is me now
   not a phase or a passing extravagance.
It has taken me over:
   I who once saw only good,
Can see only him
   in her arms.
And each kiss cuts me to the quick
   yet again.

I thought I had cried
   all of my tears,
I filled rivers and oceans
   but never the hole
That burns through my heart
   every time I think of him.
And how the sun lit his hair
   and his laughed filled a room.

What is the point of tears
   that never heal?
How could a God give us such a tool
   then make it impotent
To take away the pain
   when we need it most?
God damn him God damn him God damn
   God damn God.

Somewhere in the fog
   is my daughter -
Old in her youth,
   Young in her age.
Keeping me here
   in this world

Fredrick Hudgin

Until blessed relief rescues me
      from him.

Someday she'll be gone
      and I'll be alone,
Still wishing him here
      with me.
With memories of the times
      we laughed and we cried:
An old woman's
      last company.

Smiles

I've always been
    a sucker
For a silly smile.

The swell of a breast
    or rippling thigh
Is wonderful
    to behold, but

I've always been
    a sucker
For a silly smile.

Fredrick Hudgin

Smokin'

The thing I like least
    about your smoking
Is that I don't want
    to kiss you anymore.

Tease

There are a lot of things
      that I want to share
      with you.
They keep coming to the
      surface at the most
      inopportune times.
I was in a meeting
      with a vice-president and
Suddenly you were standing
      in front of me
      naked
      with the most seductive
      smile
      on your face.

What a tease!

If he had only known why
      I was so attentive and
That I wasn't really smiling
      at his joke.

Fredrick Hudgin

The Flight of the Eagle

So many years have passed
While I looked down,
      waiting,
      watchful,
Enjoying my peace,
      the rushing wind,
      the freedom,
      the solitude,
Living each moment with wonder
      and awe,
Growing,
      always growing.

Now you've come to fly with me
Having fought the same battles,
      doubt,
Fearing your fears
      embracing them,
      attacking them,
      enjoying them,
Sharing each moment with each other,
Knowing,
      but not knowing why.

We will fly together forever,
Seeking new horizons,
      new gifts,
Feeling the power,
      giving it,
      receiving it,
      growing it,
Waiting until the other eagles
Find us - find them,

Four Winds

Flying,
    always flying.

Fredrick Hudgin

The Gift

Get ready.
Are you ready?
Are you sure?
Because here it comes.
It's almost here.
Hold your breath.

Did you feel it?

It's not everyone
I send an
"I love you" to.

The Last Time

What a perfect evening it was,
    cool and clear,
An evening for walking
    and holding hands
    and making love.

Being with you was
    so comfortable,
Your head on my shoulder,
    my arm around your waist,
Going places
    that we'd gone before.

When we'd finally gone
    to bed
We made love that wasn't
    full of surprises
Just full of love.

I never thought it would be
    our last time.
I wish I'd known.

Fredrick Hudgin

The Lifeline

When I go up on deck
And the weather's rough,
I attach a lifeline
That's long and tough.

To keep me safe
Or haul me in
When swept overboard
By wave and wind.

I know I'm safe
When wind starts to whine.
Your counsel is my lighthouse.
Our love is my line.

As you are my life line,
I am your boat.
When waves come crashing,
I'll keep us afloat.

A team we are
Through rain and sun,
Through laughs and tears,
'Till life is done.

The wind finally calms.
The waves go to sleep.
The boat rocks a rhythm
As old as the deep.

The whales sing to us
While we make love.
The world at peace

Four Winds

Inside our cove.

Fredrick Hudgin

The Loneliest Poem in the World

Sometimes I give you a hug
and a kiss,
And say I love you,
Just because I know how good
I'd feel
If you did it to me.

The World's Shortest Love Poem

Kiss
Bliss
Miss
Wish

Fredrick Hudgin

Toxic Waste

Sadness covers me like a pall,
    lying softly on everything I do,
Weightless as the kiss of my lover
    on the lips of my best friend.

It has a life,
    becomes your wife,
Holds you tight,
    as the surgeon's knife
Cuts to the quick,
    hoping to help.

The nuclear solution
    to a broken heart.

Trouble

I knew you were trouble
    when you walked through the door.

Everyone else saw
    just a pretty face,
    a happy smile,
Someone to talk to
    for awhile.

But I saw dreams
    and hopes
    and fears,
Someone to share
    my remaining years.

But I'm not ready.
    It's been
    too soon.
I still cry
    when I see the moon.

Her shadow is a pall
    that covers
    my life.
Everything's gray,
    and pain and strife.

At least that keeps me
    from having
    to feel
The hole inside me
    that refuses to heal.

And now you're here
    smiling
    at me

Fredrick Hudgin

Turning upside down
    my reverie.

Offering nothing
    but hope
    and love.
Just the things,
    I want no part of.

Yeah, you're trouble
    I know
    you're trouble
I don't want to leave
    my guardian bubble.

And face the reality
    that she's
    gone.
Won't be back
    with the coming dawn.

Maybe it's time
    to bury
    the past
To make her a memory
    and stop hurting at last.

Release the hurt
    that protects
    me so.
From loving again
    and letting her go.

Good-bye my love
    That's all
    I can say
As I put down the hurt
    and walk away.

Hello trouble
    Going

Four Winds

my way?
My calendar's clear
the whole Damn day.

Fredrick Hudgin

Two Conversations

Hi. It was a long walk here. Have you ordered yet?
You look great.

> (I've missed you. I'm glad you could
> come. My heart leaps to the sun
> whenever I look into your eyes.)

No nothing much. I went skiing with some friends
and fell down a lot. I got really sunburned.

> (I wanted to hold you and kiss you a
> thousand times. I thought of your
> perfume and the softness of your hair.
> I've smiled all weekend remembering the
> gentle curves of your body as you walked
> across the room.)

Here's our food. So how are you doing? Did you
get some sleep yesterday?

> (Do you miss me? Do you think of me,
> too? Do you say my name when you look
> at the sun?)

Gee, that's great. I'm glad you're happy.

> (Your eyes are a spring day with white
> clouds, new grass, and lots of flowers.
> Seeing you smile was better than
> dessert.)

Well, lunch was good. I guess it's time to go. Can I
walk with you somewhere?

> (Fly free, little one. I will love you forever
> and nurture you whenever I can, for as
> long as you will let me.)

Two Edges

It is time.
You are leaving
      and won't return.
A lifetime of moments,
      one by one,
Led us here
      together,
And now
      it is time to leave.
I would go for you
      if you'd let me
But you won't
      and it's time.

I offer you
      a gift,
A two edged sword,
One that will
      cut your enemies
As easily as
      it cuts you,
A gift to use
      or discard
For as long
      as you want.

As I was given
      so I give,
A circle
      within circles.

Now go.
      And don't look back.
Nothing will be he same
      when you return.

Fredrick Hudgin

Even this gift will change
         as you do:

I love you.

Valentine

Alone.

I know what it feels like
    to be alone.

To listen to the clock
    ticking on the wall.
To hear the refrigerator
    turn on and off.

Most people have never watched
    the sun move across the floor,
Or curled up in a chair
    with a cup of coffee
    to greet the sunrise.

I wonder what you are doing
    with him now.
I imagine you laughing
    or crying
    or making love.

I get some comfort pretending
    that I am him,
Kind of a fantasy
    second chance
    that will never happen.

I hope he kisses you
    softly when you come home
And holds you when
    you tremble.

Happy Valentine,
    memory.

Fredrick Hudgin

Walking

Sometimes when we are together
Walking through the sands of time,
I take your hand,
Look in your eyes
And can't believe you're mine.

It's a long, strange road we've traveled;
Sometimes steep and covered with holes,
Sometimes smooth,
Sometimes rough,
Sometimes it hurt like Hell.

We finally found each other
Saying goodbye to a friend.
He was big as a moose
With a heart to match.
He liked that we met that day.

On clear starlit nights as I hold your hand
I see the moon in your eyes,
And see that we'll walk
Through the rest of our lives
With laughter, tears and joy.

So mote it be.

Warmth

Everyone in the bar
    thinks I'm weird
    sitting out here in
    the cold.
The fog's hiding the sun
    as they celebrate
    the passing of the week.

I can't imagine a better
    way to spend a clean suit
Than writing love poems
    to you
    on a dirty bench while
They look out at me
    and sip white wine.

But they don't love you and
    I do, and
I bet I'm warmer than
    they are.

Fredrick Hudgin

Who Needs a Reason

This morning I feel like
      crying
There's no particular reason
Except that I haven't done it
      in a while....

And I miss you
      holding me,
And telling me
      you love me,
And I'll be real glad
      when you're home.

Wish Feeling

A wish feeling,
     that's what we had.
How sad.

We planned our future
     and made love
And tried.

But that was all
     except for our
Wish.

Fredrick Hudgin

Wishes

I wish I'd said
      I love you,
Before it was true.

Because,
      you aren't here anymore
And now it is.

Words

The words are
     ringing loudly,
Tolling the end
     and the beginning,
An aural pall
     to cover our bed
Where our love once bounced
     rosey and lustful.

Fredrick Hudgin

Would You

Would you like to fall in love?
Are you lonely just like me?
Do you sleep alone with
      someone else?
Do you remember how it used to be?

I miss my heart beating faster
      when you came in the room,
My eyes misting over
      when you'd leave too soon.
I miss sailing and sharing,
      watching and caring.
I miss falling in love.

Someday I'll fall in love
      with someone lonely like me.
A person who's alone with
      someone else
A love like it's supposed to be.

I miss sending flowers
      on a rainy day,
Having to leave
      but wanting to stay,
I miss crying and holding,
      sighing and scolding.
I miss falling in love.

Wonder

So you're with her again
Instead of me,
Kissing her lips
And her breasts.

Laughing and playing
The way we used to
Before you grew bored
With trying at all.

Does she care about you
When you're not there?
Does she remember things
To tell you later?

Does she wait for your smile
Like I used to?
Does she buy little presents
To leave as surprises?

Do you care about the lies
I tell our children
When they ask
Why you're not here?

Do you wonder at the smell
As you fuck her
On the rotting corpse
Of our marriage?

It may be too late for
A resurrection
But it's not too late for
A burial.

Adieux

The book is over, the lines complete,
The stage gone silent and bittersweet.

I did my best to entertain,
To bring thee joy instead of pain.

An' if my soliloquy did offend,
Mayhaps this speech will help to mend
Those feelings of thine which to me are dear
Although why I care is not too clear.

But an' thou enjoyed this evenings repast
Please make this book not thy last.

Thy thoughts and smiles be my reward,
Except thou few whom I have bored.
To those poor souls, I bid adieux.
To the rest of you, adieux, too.

Fredrick Hudgin

I have been writing poetry and short stories since I took a Creative Writing class at Purdue University in 1967. Unfortunately, that was the only class I passed and spent the next three years in the army, including a tour in Viet Nam. After leaving the army, I earned a BS in Computer Science from Rutgers and struck off on a career as a computer programmer.

I find that my years of writing poetry have affected how I write prose. My wife is always saying to put more narrative into the story. My poetry side keeps trying to pare it down to the emotional bare bones. What I create is always a compromise between the two.

Short stories and poems of mine have been published in Biker Magazine, two compilations by Poetry.Com, The Salal Review, The Scribbler, That Holiday Feeling, a collection of Christmas short stories, and Not Your Mother's Book on Working for a Living.

My home is in Ariel, Washington, with my wife, two horses, two dogs and three cats.

My website is **fredrickhudgin.com**. All of my books and short stories are described with links to where you can buy them in hardcopy or e-book form. I've also included some of my favorite poems. You can see what is currently under development, sign up for book announcements, or volunteer to be a reader of my books that are under development.

Other books by Fredrick Hudgin:

The End of Children Trilogy – Science Fiction – Available in
paperback or e-book from Amazon

Some graduate students discover how to open a wormhole
after one of them has a dream about it. A wormhole is a hole
in our universe that goes from one place to another,
bypassing everything, including the distance. When the
students open their first wormhole, an alert is sounded by
the wormhole detectors that were planted on the moon fifty
thousand years ago. The wormhole detectors were placed
by the species that raised up humanity from apes to people.

The alert causes humanity to be evaluated by the Galactic
Species Control Board, the New Species Enforcement arm of
the Ur. The Ur is the Confederation of Sentient Species in
our galaxy. Wormholes would allow humanity to begin
spreading and exploring the rest of the galaxy. We are
evaluated to see if we have progressed enough to begin
trading and interacting with the other peaceful species who
already inhabit much of the galaxy.

The evaluation examines us to see if we have accomplished
the five basic milestones of acceptance into the UR: ending
war, controlling capitalism, ending pollution, ending
resource depletion, and ending overpopulation. We fail to
pass their evaluation. Because there is no way to stop us
from developing starships using the wormhole technology
and spreading our warlike attitudes and greed throughout
the galaxy, humanity is selected for elimination. This is done
by simply turning off our ability to have children.

The dream was planted by someone who wanted humanity
evaluated before we were ready, which would cause us to be
selected for elimination. But no one knows who or why.
Suddenly humanity is part of a who-done-it to find out who

planted the dream, why they did it, and how the elimination decree can be reversed before the last of us dies out. Without the need to preserve our world for our children, civilization begins to unravel. We plead with the Ur to give us a second chance, but no one answers our calls.

This is the story of how it all unfolds.

Book 1 – The Beginning of the End

Book 2 – The Three-Hour War

Book 3 – The Emissary

Ghost Ride – Fantasy/Action-Thriller – Available as a paperback or e-book on the Amazon web site.

A novel about how ghosts share our lives and interact with us daily

David is a Green Beret medic. At least he was for thirty years until he retired and returned to his parents' home without a clue what to do with the rest of his life. While he is trying to figure out how to recover from the violence he'd faced in Afghanistan and Iraq, he meets a woman who shows him the way then disappears. As David rebuilds his parents' home and attempts to start an emergency care clinic in his rural town, he meets the woman's granddaughter. Together they figure out how to bring down the meth lab that has poisoned their rural town, overcome state licensing regulations preventing the clinic from opening, help their friend attempt to beat his cancer, and discover David's roots buried in an Indian sweat lodge. Ghosts abound in this story of love, betrayal, supernatural guides, and unfaithful parents. The good guys aren't entirely good. The bad guys aren't entirely bad. Nothing is what it seems at first glance in Chambersville as the book leads the reader on a merry Ghost Ride.

School of the Gods – Fantasy – Available as an e-book on the Amazon Kindle web site.

A novel about the balance between good and evil.

The idea for **The School of the Gods** began with a series of "What if…"s. What if we really did have multiple lives? What if God made mistakes and learned from them? What if our spiritual goal was to become a god and it was his job to foster us while we grew? What if we ultimately became the god of our own universe, responsible for fostering our own crop of spirits to godhead? If all that were true, there would have to be a school. I mean, that's what schools do … give us the training to start a new career.

The School of the Gods is not a book about God, religious dogma, or organized religion. Instead, it's a story about Jeremiah: ex-Marine, bar fly, and womanizer. Jeremiah's life of excess leads to an untimely end. There is nothing unusual about his death other than he is the $137,438,953,472^{nd}$ person to die since the beginning of humanity. That coincidence allows Jeremiah to bypass Judgement and get a free pass into Heaven. It also begins the story.

Jeremiah's entry into the hereafter leads to him becoming the confident of the god of our universe. As Jeremiah begins his path toward godhead, he discovers the answer to many questions about God that have confounded humanity from the beginning of time like why transsexuals exist, the real reason for the ten commandments, why the Great Flood of Noah actually happened, and where all of the other species that couldn't fit on the boat were kept. Along the way, God, Jeremiah, and three other god-hopefuls throw the forces of evil out of God's Home, create a beer drinker's guide to the universes, and become all-powerful gods of their own universes.

Green Grass – Fantasy/Sci Fi – Available as an e-book on the Amazon Kindle web site.

A novel in which a magical world collides with our technological one.

It features five archeology students who find a scroll at a dig in the Dead Sea which describes in great detail how to open a portal to Paradise. Paradise has no war, crime, lawyers, or politicians. Everyone just gets along and grows together. Instead of turning the scroll over to their professor, they decide to try it and find it works. They send one of their own to Paradise and, amazingly, get someone from Paradise in return.

Once the swap happens, they learn that they can't undo it for a year. Each of the swapped students has to learn to survive in a world that is completely different from the one in which they have grown up. Paradise, as it turns out, is not the quiet nirvana that was described in the two-thousand-year-old scroll. The Earth students drop into the middle of a civil war with dragons, mages, swords, smuggled technology from Earth, and double agents on both sides of the portal.

Sulphur Springs – Historical Fiction – Available as an e-book on the Amazon Kindle web site.

A novel about two women who settle in the Northwest.

Duha (pronounced DooHa) is the daughter of a slave midwife. Her mother and she are determined to escape the racism in Independence, Missouri, by migrating to Washington State in

1895. But her mother dies in Sheridan, Wyoming, leaving Duha with no money, no job and no future but working in the brothels. She meets Georgia Prentice, a nurse in the hospital where her mother dies. Georgia takes her in and, together, they begin a life together that spans sixty years and three generations.

They settle in the quiet, idyllic settlement of Sulphur Springs, Washington, nestled between three volcanoes: Mt Rainier, Mt Adams and Mt St Helens. The beautiful fir covered hills and crystal clear rivers belie the evil growing there that threatens to swallow Duha's and Georgia's families. Three generations must join together as a psychotic rapist/murderer threatens to destroy everything that they have worked and suffered to create.

Proof

68613130R00117

Made in the USA
Charleston, SC
12 March 2017